The Story

Adam

And

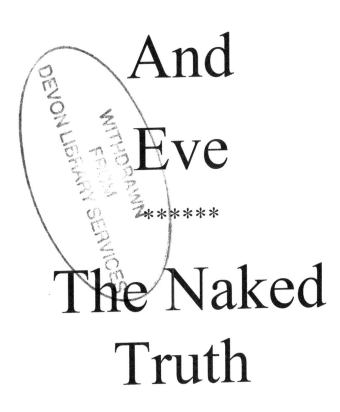

Eve

******

The Naked

Truth

By

Terry Daniels

The Naked Truth Bible Series

Book Two

terryjdaniels@gmail.com

Terry Daniels - Adam and Eve: The Naked Truth

Book Two of The Naked Truth Bible Series

Second Edition

Copyright © 2012 by Amazon Create Space Publishing

CONTENTS

Maxim: I once heard an allegory about two characters called "Truth" and "A Lie" which ended with the phrase "**Here comes the naked Truth!**" That phrase stuck with me and has become the drive for my teaching and this Bible series. Thank you, E.B. Young.

FOREWORD

Dear reader,

It is my pleasure to introduce to you "Adam and Eve: The Naked Truth," a thought-provoking and engaging book that explores one of the most intriguing stories of all time.

From the very beginning of humanity, the tale of Adam and Eve has fascinated and captivated people from all walks of life. The story of their creation, their temptation by the serpent, and their eventual expulsion from the Garden of Eden has been interpreted in countless ways, inspiring countless works of art, literature, and philosophy.

In "Adam and Eve: The Naked Truth," the authors take a fresh look at this timeless story, examining its various interpretations and shedding new light on its underlying themes and messages. Through meticulous research and insightful analysis, they guide us on a journey of discovery, exploring the complex relationship between humanity, nature, and the divine.

But this is more than just a book about theology or philosophy. It is a book that speaks to the very essence of what it means to be human. It challenges us to confront our own limitations, our own desires and fears, and our own place in the world. It reminds us that, despite our differences and imperfections, we are all part of a larger whole, bound together by our shared humanity.

As you embark on this journey, I encourage you to approach this book with an open mind and a willingness to engage with the ideas presented. Whether you are a believer or a skeptic, a scholar or a layperson, you are sure to find something of value within these pages.

So, without further ado, I invite you to join Adam and Eve on their quest for truth and understanding. May this book inspire you, challenge you, and ultimately, help you to see the world in a new and enlightening way.

May God Bless!

Chapter One

ADAM

"God is light, and in him is no darkness at all" *(1 John 1:5)* for "God is love". *(1 John 4:8)* "So God created man in his own image, in the image of God created he him." *(Gen 1:27)* "And the LORD God formed man of the dust of the ground, and breathed into his nostrils the breath of life; and man became a living soul." *(Gen 2:7)*

While still lying on the ground,

Adam began to slowly breathe on his own. As he opened his eyes for the very first time, he beheld the most beautiful sight - his awesomely powerful and compassionate Creator kneeling beside him with beams of light surrounding Him. Adam noticed that he also had the same light encircling him for man was formed in the image of God. Adam's passions, his appetites and all of his thoughts and affections were, like his Creator, pure and noble, for he bore the perfect character of his Creator because he was God's firstborn human son. No hint of darkness was found in man. *(1 John 1:5)* It's important to note here that when informed of his origin, Adam had to accept, purely by faith, everything God told him for "Man shall not live by bread alone, but by every word that proceedth out of the mouth of God." *(Matt 4:4)* That day an awesome and intimate, paternal relationship began between Adam and the God of Life, designed to last forever.

Traditional teaching is that this relationship between God and Adam was based on obedience - with God, as Creator, exercising great power and authority over the beings He creates. And, that from this position of power and authority, He has the right to command or order His created beings to do His bidding (with the threat of retribution if not obeyed). Although the Bible may appear to support this way of thinking, let's step back and take a deeper look into this relationship between God and His created beings. Let's look specifically at God's relationship with His firstborn human son, Adam.

God experiences great joy providing for and giving happiness to created beings, in this case His new human family. Notice the particular care and detail He used during Creation in preparing this world for habitation by a new race of intelligent beings. Nothing was over looked that would bring joy and happiness to man. God's greatest joy is to create intelligent beings so that they can freely enjoy, so they can freely experience, all the things He has to offer. What makes this so great is that everything He has to offer is good… all the time! That's because He is a good God…all the time!

God creates in order to give. Give what? Eternal life! Eternal life is what perfect beings experience when they exist in a perfect environment where there is no death, no darkness, and no evil, pain or suffering: the way our world was before sin. Although we are alive, what you and I are experiencing is not eternal life; we are actually experiencing death in its many forms. For instance, in God's ideal of a perfect world there no such thing as a bullet…or rape! (This will be covered more in a later chapter.)

Because God is the only Source of eternal life, when He gives life to new beings, He is giving Himself: He is literally sharing Himself with other beings so that they can experience everything that His goodness has to offer…all the time…forever! In fact, the correct definition of **Agape** (or *love*) is **selflessly giving yourself, your life, so that others can have or experience the best that life can offer…forever**.

Simplify put, this infinitely powerful God, your God, our God, as difficult as this may be to believe, is Himself a Servant; a Servant that serves up Life; a Servant that serves up Himself. God created Adam (like He did angels) so that he could experience Life, of which God is the only Source. God is Agape (*love*): a selfless servant! God is completely self-supporting so He does not need servants. *(See Acts 17:24, 25)*

When God creates a world and populates it with intelligent beings, He is growing His kingdom: He wants to serve that world by continuously giving of Himself; by infusing that environment with dynamic and exciting wonder beyond imagination. "Eye hath not seen, nor ear heard, neither have entered into the heart of man, the things which God hath prepared for them that love him." *(1 Cor 2:9)* How awesome is that!? And when He creates a being, that being, like Him, lives to serve. Hence, Adam (before the Fall) was a servant just like his Creator!

So, on that 6th day of creation, a relationship, a covenant if you will, was formed between the God of Eternal Life and Adam (who represented all humans to come). A relationship based *not* on obedience, but trust and mutual respect, with

Adam's trust in God growing infinitely with each passing second as he experienced more and more of God's goodness; and God respecting Adam's choice to continue in a relationship that God, not Adam, initiated.

And yes, Adam did have the choice to discontinue the relationship if he so chose…without reprisal! That is, without the threat of punishment. That's because even though God may desire a relationship, He gives every being the choice to be, or not be, a party in that relationship, (and that included Lucifer and angels, as well). And, that also includes you and me. "I have set before you life

and death...therefore choose life"
(Due 30:19)

God does not pull rank or coerce beings to be in a relationship with Him. Not even He can, or would ever, command or order beings to "love and serve" Him, because "love" does not work that way. Every being He creates is given freewill. God wins the affections of created being by giving of Himself, by putting before them all of His goodness, and His goodness does the rest. "Yea, I have loved thee with an everlasting love: *therefore with lovingkindness have I drawn thee." (Jer 31:3)* The reason you and I even know anything about

Him is because He is reaching out to us, "wooing" us, drawing us, by showing us samples and examples of His goodness as He ministers to us. He wants us to know that what He offers us is better than anything we have, or will ever be able to get, apart from Him.

Let me conclude this chapter by emphasizing this point: real love, and I'm talking about Agape here, is *the continual, selfless giving of one's self to improve, to better, to lift up or enhance, someone else's life experience without receiving, or expecting to receive, anything in return.* This is the way God's love, God's Goodness, works. And this is the goodness God placed in Adam when he was created. And as long as Adam chose to maintain his connection to "true vine" *(John 15:1, 4)*, continuously drawing on that Goodness, he would remain "the image of God...*forever*. And what God did on the seventh day of creation week *(Sabbath, see Gen 2:1-3)* was to ensure Adam would be granted continued free access to this Source of Life, this Source of Goodness...forever!

"Oh, taste and see that the Lord is good." *(Psalms 34:8)*

Chapter Two

EVE

So, God created them in his own image, in the image of God created he him; male and female created he them." *(Gen 1:27)*

"And the LORD God caused a deep sleep to fall upon Adam, and he slept: and he took one of his ribs, and closed up the flesh instead hereof; And the rib, which the LORD God had taken from man, made he a woman, and brought her unto the man. And Adam said, This is now bone of my bones, and flesh of my flesh: *she shall be called Woman, because she was taken out of Man."* *(Gen 2:20-23)*

"And Adam called his wife's name Eve; because she was the mother of all living." *(Gen 3:20)*

"And out of the ground the Lord God formed every beast of the field, and every fowl of the air; and brought them unto Adam to see what he would call them: and whatever Adam called every living creature, that was the name thereof." *(Gen 2:19)*

Both Adam and Eve were created on the sixth day. But it's interesting to

23

note what took place between their births. First, the Bible makes it clear that God had every intention of creating Eve. *Gen 2:18* says "And the LORD God said, It is not good that the man should be alone; I will make him an help meet for him".

In Chapter 1 we learned that God is good and everything He creates is good. But here, we have a situation that is, according to God, "not good"; or more appropriately, not complete. This was by design. In saying, "it is not good that the man should be alone", God, of course, understood this principal, but it was important that Adam understand this vital point. Something, or, in this case, someone had to be added in order for Adam (and this world) to be complete. The one thing Adam needed to be complete was Eve. So, Eve was not an afterthought, she was part of the original plan all along. A very important part of the plan, I might add.

(Note: We will discuss what both Adam and Eve needed to be complete in Chapter 4 entitled "The Covenant".)

To help Adam realize his incompleteness, his purpose, the position he will hold in this new world, God invited him to assist in naming the animals, which by the way was an exciting and glorious task: an opportunity to participate in the final phases of creation. "And out of the ground the LORD God formed every beast of the field, and every fowl of the air; and brought them unto Adam to see what he would call them: and whatsoever Adam called every living creature, that was the name thereof." *(Gen 2:19)*

At Creation, there was a harmony, an eternal connection, God, between plants, animals and man. Everything radiated Eternal Life (life without decay or death), all gave to Life, and everything perpetuated Life. Adam, with God's blessings, gave each its place in the dynamics of Life. The glory and goodness of God radiated in each blade of grass or with each low of the calf. But, as enjoyable, attentive and responsive nature was to his voice and his touch, Adam soon realized that nature could not fully appreciate the wonders of God; that nature could not fully appreciate the gifts God had given him. Adam realized he needed a mate; one who could recognize the fullness of God's goodness, and one who could meet or fulfill his greatest need - the need to serve.

Everything went just the way God intended. Adam, like his Creator, was a selfless servant, and God wanted Adam to feel what it's like to have this powerful drive to enhance the lives of others.

"And Adam gave names to all cattle, and to the fowl of the air, and to every beast of the field; but for Adam

there was not found an <u>help meet</u> for him." *(Gen 2:20)* Now, Adam understands why God creates worlds, and that is so He can bless or minister to others. Because Adam now deeply realizes his greatest need is to serve, God can now supply that need by creating Eve.

"And the LORD God caused a deep sleep to fall upon Adam, and he slept: and he took one of his ribs, and closed up the flesh instead thereof. And the rib, which the LORD God had taken from man, made he a woman, and brought her unto the man. And Adam said, "This is now bone of my bones, and flesh of my flesh: she shall be called Woman, because she was taken out of Man." *(Gen 2:21-23)*

God prepared Adam for this very moment. He groomed him to be the joy of Eve's life. Now it was on! She was to be the recipient of every good and precious gift that Adam's glorious mind could conceive.

Adam could hardly contain his joy. "This is now bone of my bones." Eve will now have two special beings in her life, her loving Father and her attentive husband. She will daily give praises for every wonderful act Adam performs on her behalf. And Adam will give praises to his Creator for the acts of Agape (continual selfless service to enhance the life of others) that he will gladly perform for his wife. (Note: Eve was a gifted servant, too; so, take a moment, allow your mind to explore the infinite possibilities of how awesome and wonderful the experience would be for both Adam and Eve!)

The harmony in the new world spoke to this newly married pair of God's infinite wisdom and power. They were ever discovering some new attraction that filled their hearts with deeper agape and called forth renewed expressions of gratitude. So long as they continued to draw from the Source of Life, their capacity to know, to enjoy, and to bless and serve each other would grow continually. They would be constantly gaining new treasures of knowledge, discovering fresh springs of happiness, and obtaining clearer and yet clearer conceptions of the immeasurable, unfailing love of God.

"And they were both naked, the man and his wife, and were not ashamed.

Thus the heavens and the earth were finished, and all the host of them. And God saw everything He had made, and, behold, it was very good." *(Gen 2:25, 1; 1:31)*

This, of course, was God's original plan.

Chapter Three

THE CORONATION

Definitions:

Coronation: The ceremony of crowning a sovereign.

Sovereign: One that exercises supreme authority within a limited sphere.

"And God said, Let us make man in our image, after our likeness: and let them have dominion over the fish of the sea, and over the fowl of the air, and over the cattle, and over all the earth, and over every creeping thing that creepeth upon the earth." *(Gen 1:26)*

"What is man, that thou art mindful of him? or the son of man that thou visitest him? Thou madest him a little lower than the angels; [then] thou crownedst him with glory and honour, and didst set him over the works of thy hands: Thou hast put all things in subjection under his feet. For in that he put all under the sovereignty of man: he left nothing outside his control." *(Heb 2:6-8)*

Adam was God's firstborn human son, and "first fruit" and "seed" of the human race: which simply means that he was the first, and source, of many more to come. But God had greater plans in store for Adam. The scriptures say that after he was made "a little lower than the angels", God "crowned him with glory and honor." *(Heb 2:7)* In God's infinite wisdom Adam was given total sovereignty over the newest world in God's ever-expanding kingdom. No angel, including Lucifer, had ever been honored to such a degree! "For though in past ages God did grant authority to angels, yet he did not put [a] future world…under their control, and it is this world that we are now talking about." *(Heb 2:5)*

Amazing! A human given power and authority higher than angels! And, as awesome as this may sound, please don't miss the point that Adam was given, as sovereign and king of his own domain, supreme authority to determine the eternal future of the new world *("By one man...", Rom 5:12)*. Talk about being crowned with "glory and honor"!

This revelation should raise a myriad of questions such as "why would God this?" or "what does all of this mean?" And, as we look at the history of our world and the shape it is in today, we might even wonder if granting Adam these extraordinary privileges was a wise decision.

Honestly speaking, I can't answer the first two questions whether God granting Adam these privileges was wise decision. The Bible tells us that God is the source of wisdom:"For the LORD giveth wisdom: out of his mouth cometh knowledge and understanding." *(Prov 2:6)* So, I accept, by faith, that God setting Adam up this way, was indeed, a wise decision, even if I don't understand it.

Would Adam live up to this awesome privilege?

Chapter Four

THE COVENANT

In this chapter we will explore the everlasting covenant agreement between God, Adam and Eve that was to shape the eternal future of the world.

"And God said, Let us make man in our image, after our likeness: and let them have dominion over the fish of the sea, and over the fowl of the air, and over the cattle, and over all the earth, and over every creeping thing that creepeth upon the earth. So God created man in his own image, in the image of God created he him; male and female created he them. And God blessed them, and God said unto them, Be fruitful, and multiply, and replenish the earth, and subdue it: and have dominion over the fish of the sea, and over the fowl of the air, and over every living thing that moveth upon the earth." *(Gen 1:26-28)*

"Reproduce! Fill the Earth! Take ownership!" *(Vs. 28)*

Gen 2:1, 2 states, "Thus the heavens and the earth were finished, and all the host of them. And on the seventh day God ended his work which he had made; and he rested on the seventh day from all his work which he had made." The idea here is that

God completed His work of creating and populating the new world, and that's correct. But, was the work of creating actually complete?

It's clear that 1) In six days God created "the heavens and the earth" 2) On the sixth day He created two human citizens, and 3) On the seventh day He ended His work of creating a new world populated with two humans. That being said, I ask - was this the end goal? According to *Gen 1:28* - where Gods instructs Adam and Eve to "Reproduce! Fill the Earth! Take ownership!" - the apparent answer is no!

Note that God ended His work on the seventh day but His charge for Adam and Eve to "Reproduce!" and "Fill the Earth!" happened on the sixth day of creation which leads us to examine the special circumstance or *covenant* put in place on sixth day: Adam and Eve were blessed with the great honor of completing the creation experience! Yes, God's work did end on the seventh day but Adam and Eve's work of creating was just beginning!

Clearly God, with His creative powers, could have easily filled the earth with His new human family but purposely turned this responsibility over to Adam and Eve as sovereigns (having dominion) over the new world. And, Adam and Eve to accomplish the task of populating the new world, God invested them with His power to create...life! First, a perfect God created two perfect human beings. Now this perfect God passed the gift to create life to two perfect humans with the goal that they create a world full of perfect humans.

This was the covenant plan. And this covenant agreement Adam and Eve initially accepted!

Chapter Five

THE WARNING

You may recall that in chapter 3, *"The Coronation"*, we discovered that Adam, though made "a little lower than the angels" *(Heb 2:7)*, was "crowned" with honor higher than that of any angel: Also given complete sovereignty over the newest world in God's kingdom. *(Gen 1:26; Heb 2:8)* And, with that honor, Adam was granted the power to determine the eternal future of earth and its inhabitants.

And, in chapter 4, "The Covenant", we learned that God placed in Adam's seed and Eve's womb a gift that God alone possesses: the power to create life! We also learned why: In God's charge to "Reproduce! Fill the Earth! Take ownership!" *(Vs. 28)*, a perfect God passed to a perfect Adam and Eve the privilege of completing earth's creation process – filling this world with perfect humans. A work that God could have easily done but He passed this honor to Adam and Eve. He transferred this honor in the form of an eternal agreement; an everlasting covenant between God and the two representatives of His future human family. A covenant agreement that Adam and Eve initially accepted.

So, it was with great amazement when their Creator lovingly informed them that it was their privilege, their right, to, at any time they so desired, opt out of their eternal, covenant relationship with Him. That is, if they ever choose to live apart from God, to sever their eternal connection to Him, they could do so *without reprisal from God.* This right, this privilege is afforded to every intelligent being God creates as a member of His family - even Lucifer and the angels!

Adam and Eve's response to this announcement was one of astonishment. They could not fathom anybody ever wanting to sever their eternal connection to God. "Who would ever want to leave His presence?" they whispered.

God does not force, demand or command allegiance. The beings that abide in His presence do so solely because they desire to do so. Not because they are afraid of punishment, but because they trust Him. And they see in Him the best that Life has to offer, and they desire, above all else, to ever to be in His presence and to bathe in the richness of His Glory.

"Abide in me, and I in you. As the branch cannot bear fruit of itself, except it abide in the vine; no more can ye, except ye abide in me. I am the vine, ye are the branches: He that abideth in me, and I in him, the same bringeth forth much fruit: for without me ye can do nothing. If a man abide not in me, he is cast forth as a branch, and is withered; and men gather them, and cast them into the fire, and they are burned." *(John 15:4-6)*

"And the LORD God took the man, and put him into the Garden of Eden to dress it and to keep it. And the LORD God commanded the man, saying, Of every tree of the garden thou mayest freely eat: But of the tree of the knowledge of good and evil, thou shalt not eat of it: for in the day that thou eatest thereof thou shalt surely die." *(Gen 2:15-17)*

In making this announcement, God was not only informing the holy pair of their rights, He was also attempting to open their understanding to the horrible consequences that would result from severing their ties to Him, the only Source of Life. The "tree of the knowledge of good and evil" was obviously no ordinary tree. As it turns out it was a tree that would set one free: not from jail or prison – but from God! A tree that would close off one to goodness and expose them to evil - permanently cutting one off from the Source of Life! Alive…but dead! Dead to God and His family/kingdom.

So, when God said, "in the day that thou eatest thereof *thou shalt surely die*", this was not a pronouncement of punishment; God was trying to explain to them that apart from Him there is no life, nothing good – only evil, "for without me ye can do nothing." *(John 15:5)*

In God's vision for all life, His greatest desire is that no being he creates ever come to know evil, in any of its many forms – pain, suffering, death, etc.

Simply put, God asks free beings to believe, abide and trust Him with their lives, and embrace His promise that they would be rewarded greatly throughout eternity. So, every being (angel or human) has to decide for themselves if they want to live (abide) within the bounds of God's government, or not.

Again, Adam and Eve whispered, "Who would ever want to leave His presence?"

But what this holy couple did not know is that one being had already exercised his right to exist apart from God, and was, even then, meticulously urging other angels to do the same. So, included in the announcement was a warning about this uprising. God, along with the angels, began to warn earth's first inhabitants that questions were being raised about God's government and character by Lucifer's alter-ego, Satan!

The holy pair could not understand why God would allow this action by any of His created beings, showing they still did not understand the freedom of choice afforded each being. Everyone has a right to state his case to whoever will listen, and, with the listener the right is given to decide for themselves what's true. So, God and the holy angels did everything possible to prepare Adam and Eve for their inevitable encounter with the author lies and confusion.

In conclusion, in placing *"the tree of the knowledge of good and evil"* in the garden, God had in mind a fourfold purpose for Adam and Eve. 1) to inform them that by eating from the tree they could opt out of their eternal relationship with God at any time, without retribution; 2) to warn them of the horrible consequences that comes with that choice; 3) to warn them that one being had exercised his choice to leave God's governing influence and was, at that very moment, experiencing (and demonstrating) the dangerous effects that choice was having on him; and 4) which was most important: God made sure that Adam and Eve understood that to eat from *"the tree of the knowledge of good and evil"* would be their acknowledgment to God their decision to sever all ties believing that there was something better for them apart from God. The choice would be theirs alone.

After the warning, God must step back and allow the growing

rejection to continue. Why? Because at the heart of this work were claims that God could not be trusted and questions about His goodness were being raised. God must allow every being the opportunity to hear and then to decide the validity of these claims. That would include Adam and Eve, for they too, must be allowed to hear these claims and then decide, for themselves, if they were true or not. In the end, every human born on this planet will have had to face the same decision. Beginning with Cain, we each will have to, after hearing all the chatter about God (true or false, good and bad, right or wrong), make up our own minds about Him. About His word. Pray to God that you get access to the correct information! Your (eternal) life depends on it!

"Let every man be fully persuaded in his own mind." *(Rom 14:5)*

Chapter Six

THE TEMPTATION

"And the LORD God commanded the man, saying, Of every tree of the garden thou mayest freely eat: But of the tree of the knowledge of good and evil, thou shalt not eat of it: for in the day that thou eatest thereof thou shalt surely die." *(Gen 2:16, 17)*

"How art thou fallen from heaven, O Lucifer, son of the morning! how art thou cut down to the ground,

which didst weaken the nations!"
(Isa 14:12)

"Now the serpent was more subtle than any beast of the field which the LORD God had made. And he said unto the woman, Yea, hath God said, ye shall not eat of every tree of the garden? And the woman said unto the serpent, we may eat of the fruit of the trees of the garden: But of the fruit of the tree which is in the

midst of the garden, God hath said, Ye shall not eat of it, neither shall ye touch it, lest ye die. And the serpent said unto the woman, Ye shall not surely die: For God doth know that in the day ye eat thereof, then your eyes shall be opened, and ye shall be as gods, knowing good and evil." *(Gen 3:1-5)*

How appropriate it is that the scriptures show the depths of Lucifer's fall from his high and holy position - to that of a "serpent" (or snake). How much lower could he possibly go? Or, as *Isa 4:12* so fitly puts it, "How art thou fallen from heaven, O Lucifer, son of the morning! how art thou cut down to the ground". At this point, the only person Lucifer is concerned about is himself. In fact, the Bible no longer refers to him as Lucifer, but as

Satan, or the Devil: for you see, he is no longer an angel of light. And, it's important to note that, although they occupy the same body, Lucifer and Satan are two *totally different*, *completely opposite*, beings. God created Lucifer, an angel of light! Lucifer, by his choice to be free from God, became Satan, angel of darkness! Lucifer was indeed dead! *("If you don't stay joined to me, you will be like a branch that has been thrown out...and dies!" John 15:6)*

Now, we find the fallen being, Satan, in the Garden of Eden engaged in conversation with Eve, speaking to her through a snake (serpent). It's vital to pay close attention to the dialogue because the meaning behind the dialogue is very important. It's also important to know up front that Satan's objective is to create doubt in the minds of Adam and Eve about God's word, goodness and trustworthiness, and about the wonderful relationship they had with the Creator.

"And he said unto the woman, Yea, hath God said, ye shall not eat of every tree of the garden?" In asking this question, Satan is questioning God's word. If God is good and, everything He creates is good, then every tree in the Garden of Eden should be good and available. Obviously, he knew the terrible results eating from the *"tree of the knowledge of good and evil"* would bring and wanted to create doubt about God's promises (word) for those who remain citizens of His eternal family/kingdom.

"And the woman said unto the serpent, we may eat of the fruit of the trees of the garden: But of the fruit of the tree which is in the midst of the garden, God hath said, Ye shall not eat of it, neither shall ye touch it, lest ye die." *(Gen 3:2, 3)*

Eve's response shows, at this point, she understood and trusted God's word about the damage eating from the tree would cause: death! (Alive but eternally cutoff (dead) to God and His kingdom!) But in Satan's reply, *"Ye shall not surely die"*, he was saying that God's word was a lie, implying that there is, indeed, life apart from God (which is truly a lie!) Satan adds, "For God doth know that in the day ye eat thereof, then your eyes shall be opened, and ye shall be as gods, knowing good and evil".

As stated earlier, God's greatest desire is that none ever experience the horrors of evil, and that abiding in Him is the only way to avoid such a fate. On the other hand, Satan's greatest desire is to destroy lives: like he did to his own. So, he says to Eve, "For God doth know that in the day ye eat thereof, then your eyes shall be opened, and ye shall be as gods, knowing good and evil" *(Gen 3:6)*. Here Satan is saying that - God's claim - that eating from the tree would permanently close one's eyes to goodness and permanently open one's eyes to evil - was not true. Satan was also saying that *knowing evil* was good thing – the complete opposite of God's word! All in an attempt to convince Adam and Eve that something actually wonderful would happen if they eat from the tree.

God, prior to the meeting between Satan and humans, tried to convince Adam and Eve to trust His word…no matter what! "Abide in Me", He says. "Never take the horrible step of separating yourselves from Me", warning them of the pain and woe they would experience if they do. And that He had always been upfront and honest with them. But at this point, He has to let both Adam and Eve choose who they were going to believe: God or Satan. God said knowing evil would be a bad decision: Satan claimed it would be a good one.

"And when the woman saw that the tree was good for food, and that it was pleasant to the eyes, and a tree to be desired to make one wise, she took of the fruit thereof, and did eat, and gave also unto her husband with her; and he did eat." *(Gen 3:6)*

Unfortunately, Eve chose to believe Satan – not God!

And so, with the excitement of a child on Christmas morning, "she took of the fruit thereof, and did eat". She notices that she is still breathing so she reasons that Satan was telling the truth and that God had lied! Then she *"gave also unto her husband with her; and he did eat"*. Because Eve is still breathing, Adam now believes God's word cannot be trusted.

And so, Adam, believing Satan's lie

makes the plunge into darkness. "And the eyes of them both were opened." (Gen 3:7) Eyes now opened to evil, pain and suffering for the rest of their lives…taking the entire human race with them. "By one man [and woman] sin entered into the world…and death." *(Rom 5:12)* Mercy!

Chapter Seven

THE FALL

"And the eyes of them both were opened, and they knew that they were naked; and they sewed fig leaves together, and made themselves aprons." *(Gen 3:7)* "And the LORD God said, Behold, the man is become as one of us, to know good and evil." *(Gen 3:22)*

The reality of God's words "ye shall surely die" *(Gen 2:17)* had taken effect - even though Adam and Eve may not have, of yet, fully realized the magnitude of those words. They were alive but were things still the same? Had they indeed severed all ties to God's kingdom of total light and goodness - as He had promised? And like Satan, were they now engulfed in total darkness? Here are a few texts:

"Now we see through a glass darkly." *(1 Cor 13:12)*

"And [Moses] said, I beseech thee, shew me thy glory…And [God] said, Thou canst not see my face: for there shall no man see me, and live." *(Ex 33:18, 20)*

"There is no fear of God before their eyes." *(Rom 3:1)*

"Having eyes full of adultery, and that cannot cease from sin." *(2 Pet 2:14)*

"Having eyes, see ye not." *(Mark 8:8)*

"There is none righteous, no, not one." *(Rom 3:10)*

"For all that is in the world, the lust of the flesh, and the lust of the eyes, and the pride of life, is not of the Father, but is of the world." *(1 John 2:16)*

"The heart is deceitful above all

things, and desperately wicked:
who can know it?" *(Jer 17:9)*

"The lamp of the body is the eye. If your eye is sound, your whole body will be full of light. But if your eye is evil, your whole body will be full of darkness. If all the light you have is darkness, it is dark indeed!" *(Matt 6:22, 23)*

"Now we see through a glass darkly." *(1 Cor 13:12)*

"And God shall wipe away all tears from their eyes." *(Rev 21:4)*

Yes, Adam and Eve's "eyes were opened" but tragically they are now open to see things that God hoped they would never, ever see. Horrible things! Terrible things! Deadly things! "If you don't remain attached to me, you will be like a branch that has fallen from the tree and died." *(John 15:6)*

The fact that they were "naked" and, that they could see that they were naked, meant that they no longer possessed the purity of life eternal. God was still full of life but because Adam and Eve were now empty (naked)!

"And they heard the voice of the LORD God walking in the garden in the cool of the day: and Adam and his wife hid themselves from the presence of the LORD God amongst the trees of the garden. And the LORD God called unto Adam, and said unto him, Where art thou? And he said, I heard thy voice in the garden, and I was afraid, because I was naked; and I hid myself." *(Gen 3:8, 9, 10)*

Here, we see Adam and Eve hiding…from God. Created to dwell in the presence of Selfless Love throughout eternity, they are now "afraid" and ashamed to even be near Him. When God said, *"for in the day that thou eatest thereof thou shalt surely die"*, He was not speaking of some future event as some teach: He meant the actual moment Adam and Eve ate from the tree, (thereby severing their relationship with Him), they would die…that day! The *"surely"* meant they could be absolutely sure that it would happen: They could bank on it! And, *that very day*, they did, indeed, die! All the good, all the Light, the Life, the Agape, that God had placed in them, in their minds, in their thoughts, at creation, vanished…and was replaced with darkness.

To further illustrate:

"And he (God) said, Who told thee that thou wast naked? Hast thou eaten of the tree, whereof I commanded thee that thou shouldest not eat? And the man said, The woman whom thou gavest to be with me, she gave me of the tree, and I did eat." *(Gen 3:11, 12)*

God was not seeking answers when He asked these questions because He is all-knowing. This was God's first attempt at redemption in trying to move the, now, un-holy pair, to self-examination, and then, to repentance. This was His first attempt to pierce their *now* darkened state of mind, because a person in darkness is incapable, on his own, of seeing the depths of his condition (e.g., humans).

To demonstrate the depth of Adam's darkened state, the Bible goes on to say, *"And the man said, The woman whom thou gavest to be with me, she gave me of the tree, and I did eat"* *(Gen 3:12)*. Note that Adam speaks first, not to protect or clear his wife of any responsibility for what happened, but to implicate her. There was a time when Adam felt extremely blessed to have this woman, even calling her "bone of my bone and flesh of my flesh". Now, he's trying to distance himself from her because he is seeking to protect himself, for you see, he is no longer a selfless being and now he cares about serving no one but himself. He has no problem implicating, blaming, someone else.

Furthermore, in an attempt to remove all blame from himself, Adam says to God, *"the woman whom <u>thou</u> gavest to be with me"*, trying to blame, and, to distance himself from God, too. At this point, Adam cares about no one but himself.

Initially, Adam was created to be Eve's servant: but God says to Eve, now "he shall rule over thee", *(Gen 3:16)* God, here, was not administering punishment on Eve (or women); He was stating a fact. The happy state of marriage they were to have experienced was now eternally gone: Adam and Eve were no longer *sinless or selfless* equals.

Now, Eve (along with women in general), were going to experience selfish, corrupt men trying to rule over them!

The fall was so devastating that God, speaking to Satan, says in *Gen 3:15*, "And I will put enmity between thee and the woman, and between thy seed and her seed". In the Clear Word Bible translation, it reads, "*I will place a hatred of sin in the heart of the woman **and** her descendants*". Notice that the fall did not only affect Adam and his wife, Eve, but "*her descendants*" as well. "Wherefore, as *by one man sin entered into the world, and death by sin; and so death passed upon all* men"; "For...in Adam all die"; "There is none righteous, no, not one." (Rom 5:12; 1 Corinthians 15:22; Rom 3:10)

All humans have been horribly affected. And, the fall was so deep, and human's love for evil so great, so pervasive, that God had to put a restraint on its debilitating effects, for had He not done so, our sinfulness, our darkness, would have completely eradicated the entire human race from existence. This is something God does not want to happen because He has other plans, better plans, for the now fallen human race. However, because of Adam, the human race, instead of enjoying the sinless wonders of Life in God's kingdom, is now _condemned_ to this state of darkness and death (albeit held in check by God). And this _condemned state of human woe_ is an eternal one, that is, in and of itself, it has no end. If not for God's involvement in human affairs, the human race would be eternally lost and without hope!

So, with one lie, "Ye shall not surely die: For God doth know that in the day ye eat thereof, then your eyes shall be opened, and ye shall be as gods, knowing good and evil", Satan was able to convince earth's first parents that God was not truthful, and thereby, could not be trusted, *and* that "knowing good *and evil*" would not only elevate them to a higher plain, but that this new state would be exciting and exhilarating and more wonderful than anything they had experienced with God. Of course, Satan knew that this was a lie. Unfortunately, Adam and Eve would come to realize it, too!

Chapter Eight

THE AFTERMATH

"So God created them in his own image, in the image of God created he him; male and female created he them." *(Gen 1:27)*

At Creation God crowned Adam, His firstborn human son, with great power and authority above Lucifer or angels: He gave Adam sovereignty (kingship/dominion) over earth. *(See Heb 2:7, 8)* This means that God transferred to Adam the authority to determine earth's eternal future. Also, in given Adam and Eve power to create life, God also entered into a covenant agreement with both given them the honor of completing the creation process by giving life to a world full of human beings born of God's royal bloodline. *(See Chapters 3 and 4)* Perfect humans creating perfect humans! That was the plan!

Its mind boggling to think that perfect humans, choosing to believe a lie instead believing God's word, irreparably ruined that plan…and an entire world!

Definition:

Irreparable - impossible to rectify or repair.

In a way, I kind of get it: God sees everyone He creates as royal lineage (*branches of the "True Vine" (John 15:4)*, and His desire is for this relationship to continue throughout eternity. Yet, every "branch" has the right to permanent sever that royal connection if they so choose. Of course, God warns that apart from Him there is nothing good – only ruin and death *(See Gen 2:1; John 15:5, 6)*. Ignoring God's word, Adam and Eve choose, like Lucifer, eternal separation from God resulting in them all becoming dark, empty shells of what they were created to be. Now, it was their lot to live out the remainder of their horrible existence isolated from God, His noble family/kingdom, and everything that's good. It was their choice to make – now they must live (die) with that decision.

Unfortunately, the story gets worse: Even in their now God-less state, naked, void of any righteousness and eternally cutoff from God's royal bloodline – Adam and Eve still possessed the power to create life, to have children under these horrible circumstances.

"Unto the woman [God] said, I will greatly multiply thy sorrow and thy conception; in sorrow thou shalt bring forth children." *(Gen 3:16)*

Here, God is preparing Eve for what child bearing will be like now in this darkened state. Created to be the mother of God's newest, royal family members, she will now "sorrowfully" bare children that will be born "wretched, and miserable, and poor, and blind, and naked!" *(Rev 3:17)* Children born with no knowledge of God or His kingdom, or of what a world free from sin looks like. We are those children!

Some teach, and many believe, that "we are made in God's image": Scripture disagrees: "There is none righteous, no not one!" *(Rom 3:10)* If our eyes were not shrouded in darkness, we would be able to see what this text is actually saying: "There is none like God – No Not One!" As an example, take Adam and Eve's first child, Cain: what is the one thing we know about him? He was a murderer! How much like God was he? "Whosoever is born of God doth not commit sin: for [God's] seed remaineth in him." *(1 John 3:9)* Cain's problem is that his father, Adam, forsook *"God's seed"* when he ate from the tree, which means Adam could only pass to Cain (and the rest of us, as well) his own corrupted seed. Not God's! (Sigh!)

So, I ask, how many of us have seen God face to face? Adam and Eve did! That's because they were made in God's image: born of *"God's seed"*. Their children, on the other hand, did not have that privilege. (Though it was God's original intent that we would!) Sadly, we are the image of Satan – not God! We are the one's taking the brunt of Adam and Eve's choice! We didn't choose this type of life – they did; unfortunately, we are the ones suffering the consequences!

So! Believing a lie did cause all of this! (Look at earth's history in totality.) And, yes, believing the truth (trusting what God said) could have avoided this whole experience. At the end of the day, though, we are all still here, trapped in a world of darkness, without any control, whatsoever, over the outcome. It brings to mind the words of the apostle Paul: "O wretched man that I am! Who shall deliver me from the body of this death?" *(Rom 7:23)*

So, is there a way out? Or, are we ever to continue this perpetual merry-go-round of what we call life? Where: we are conceived, possibly born, maybe aborted; born with ten toes and fingers, born with a defect, born with a defect of character; born to a good family, born to a bad one, raised in foster care; educated by street gangs, educated in the best private schools; go to college, go to prison, go to war; become a hero, killed in action, end up on wall street, end up sleeping on the street; become a mother, become a father, bury our child; become a preacher, become a rapist, get Aids; die young, die old, have more children, which then starts up the merry-go-round, again! I say "there's got to be something better!" Thank God, there is!

Chapter Nine

THE PLAN

"As by one man sin entered into the world...as the offence, so also is the free gift. For if through the offence of one [man] many be dead, much more the grace of God, and the gift by grace, which is by one man, Jesus Christ, hath abounded unto many." *(Rom 5:12, 15)*

"Jesus answered and said unto him, Verily, verily, I say unto thee, Except a man be born again, he cannot see the kingdom of God." *(John 3:3)*

The plans for this world originated in the heart of the Godhead. "For there are three that bear record in heaven, the Father, the Word, and the Holy Ghost: and these three are one...the Godhead bodily...All things were made by him; and without him was not anything made that was made...And God saw everything that he had made, and, behold, it was very good." *(1 John 5:7; Col 2:9; John 1:3; Gen 1:31)*

"Very good" was the goal: A gloriously flawless world filled with God-like humans who were to be the newest members born into God's royal family bloodline.

(Branches connected to the True Vine – John 15:1, 4) Unfortunately, God's intended goal…has yet to be realized!

We learned in chapter four that although God ended His portion of creation on the Seventh Day, it was on the Sixth Day that He shared with Adam and Eve they would be honored with the covenant privilege of completing earth's creation: populating the whole earth by passing God's seed to their children. And though the holy pair initially agreed to honor this glorious task, they ultimately chose a path that would ruin God's plans for this earth: They choose to eat from "the tree of the knowledge of good and evil" *(Gen 2:1)*, rejecting God's warning that to do so would permanently sever them (and their children) from both His bloodline and kingdom, resulting in devastation for the human race.

Also, even though both made the decision, the Bible makes it clear that Adam's decision to cut ties with God is the reason for human woe, "by one man sin entered into the world." *(Rom 5:12)* That's because as God's firstborn son, it was Adam's birthright, given him at his birth, to carry and pass God's seed to every child conceived in Eve's womb. And, this plan would work only as Adam remained connected to God. Once disconnected from God, both the privilege (and God's seed) would vanish from the human experience…immediately!

As it turns out Adam did the unthinkable – he cut ties to God's seed, and locked himself, and his children (us), out of God's kingdom. This is bad news because it was God's desire to see His "seed" shared in both Adam *and* his descendants *(1 John 3:9)*. The good news, though, is that God was more than prepared! He has not given up on His plans to spend eternity with humans "born of His seed". But, in Adam, this is no longer a possibility! God will turn to another human to make that happen – Jesus!

"For if through the offence of one [man] many be dead, much more the grace of God, and the gift by grace, which is by one man, Jesus Christ, hath abounded unto many." *(Rom 5:15)*

One human male caused the problem – only a human male can address it. That's because humanity's problem and its solution is found in the "seed" of two completely different men! Make no mistake about it, sin is definitely the "elephant in the room" when discussing the human dilemma of pain and suffering! What we've failed to understand is sin's cause: Note that God did not create sinners. According to Bible, Adam did! *("by one man sin entered into the world", Rom 5:12)* Our sin problem is a result of Adam's corrupted seed being passed to his descendants through his corrupted bloodline. Tragically, we are all products of Adam's Godless seed! And there's nothing we can do about it!

Enter Jesus!

What makes Jesus different? – he's the only human born into this world *not* conceived with Adam's corrupted seed. "Behold, a virgin shall be with child, and shall bring forth a son...for that which is conceived in her is of the Holy Ghost." *(Matt 1:38, 37)* Jesus was conceived by the Holy Spirit: He is literally God's biological human son...born of God's bloodline. Simply put, he was born of God's seed – not Adams! And "Whosoever is born of God doth not commit sin; for [God's] seed remaineth in him: and he cannot sin, because he is born of God." *(1 John 3:9)* Jesus, was indeed, different, and this is "very good" news for us (Adam's descendants)!

Another important thing to know about Jesus: He has inherited the title of God's firstborn human son – the roll Adam renounced when he severed his bloodline connection to God. So, all the noble plans that God has for the human race will now flow thru Jesus.

Adam was given the privilege and power to birth us into the Father's family, but he failed to do so. The good news is that God has given Jesus the power to do the same! In Jesus, we have been given the chance to be born again: a do over. And, in his own words, Jesus makes clear that "Except a man be born again, he cannot see the kingdom of God...born again, not of corruptible seed, but of incorruptible". *(John 3:3; 1 Pet 1:23)* Also, "Except a man be born of water and of the Spirit [i.e., 'born of God'], he cannot enter into the kingdom of God" *(John 3:5; 1 John 3:9)* He is talking literal birth, not figurative (or spiritual).

New birth is a reality...in Jesus. "Nicodemus saith unto [Jesus], How can a man be born when he is old? can he enter the second time into his mother's womb, and be born?" *(John 3:4)*

When Jesus informed Nicodemus of the glorious phenomenon of new birth, Nicodemus thought it was foolishness. What about you?

Chapter Ten

CONCLUSION

Adam's "corrupted seed", passed to his descendants, has us imprisoned in a world of darkness, forever locked out of God's kingdom: Jesus is our only hope of ever seeing God face to face!

"Let not your heart be troubled: ye believe in God, believe also in me. In my Father's house are many mansions: if it were not so, I would have told you. I go to prepare a place for you. And if I go and prepare a place for you, I will come again, and receive you unto myself; that where I am, there ye may be also…I am the way, the truth, and the life: no man cometh unto the Father, but by me." *(John 14:1-3, 6)*

"The Lord is not slack concerning his promise, as some men count slackness; but is longsuffering to us-ward, not willing that any should perish, but that all should come to repentance." *(2 Pet 3:9)*

"Grace be to you and peace from God the Father, and from our Lord Jesus Christ, Who gave himself for our sins, that he might deliver us from this present evil world, according to the will of God and our Father." *(Gal 1:3, 4)*

This book was written to set the record straight about the story of Adam and Eve. So, here it is:

Because of Adam, humans have a bloodline problem: We are completely void of God's royal DNA (Genetics)! Not one drop! We manifest this reality by sinful thoughts and deeds! "For all have sinned...there is none righteous, no not one." Rom 3:23, 10) And there's nothing that can be done about our genetics: "Can the Ethiopian change his skin, or the leopard his spots?" *(Jer 13:23)* You're either born of royal blood...or not. We were not!

So, here's a great truth: As Adam's descendants, we did not choose this wretched state - Adam and Eve did – and then they passed it to their unsuspecting descendants without us having a say so in the matter. The good news is that God has a glorious solution that He, and only He, can pull off: A chance to start over from scratch (from conception)! It's called New Birth!

When Jesus said to Nicodemus "you must be born again" to see God's kingdom, Nicodemus thought Jesus was playing with his mind: "Nicodemus saith unto [Jesus], How can a man be born when he is old? can he enter the second time into his mother's womb, and be born?" *(John 3:4)* I love Jesus' response: "Jesus answered and said unto him, You're a respected teacher of Israel and you don't know these basics?" *(v. 10)* Don't miss the point: Jesus is saying that as a teacher of the scriptures, Nicodemus should have already known about new birth. Why didn't he know. Do you?

New birth is not a spiritual concept – it is a literal one. God's solution is to give all of Adam's descendants another chance to be born – the royal way this time. God's plan, His plea, is that we surrender (this horrible life we got from Adam) to the Lamb of God, and let him set us free from this world – and most importantly, from our first birth! In return, you will receive from the Lamb a brand new, royal born, life! – at his second coming! As a result, you will, for the first time, have the glorious privilege of seeing God face to face! Amen!!! (Note: The process is called Repentance.)

New birth is God's plan for Adam's godless children (if we so choose!). Nicodemus, the Bible teacher, apparently hadn't heard. I suspect he is not the only one. How about you. With all the different narrative out there, where do you stand?

Have you surrendered your life to the Lamb? He, in turn, has promised to 1) deliver you from this evil world; 2) give you a new life, a royal one; and 3) give you a mansion in his Father's house. Please do so today! Amen!

Links:

Books in "The Naked Truth Bible Series":

Electronic (Kindle, Nook, etc.):

Book One: Is God Really Good?

Book Two: Adam and Eve: The Naked Truth

Book Three: God's Law Exposed

Paperback:

Is God Really Good?

Adam and Eve: The Naked Truth

God's Law Exposed

Email Address:

Terryjdanies@gmail.com

ACKNOWLEDGMENTS

Thanks to my wife Barbara for her patience through the years, especially over the last year while God was leading me in the direction of writing. The primary burden of support for our family fell on her shoulders, and she has, with much help from God, handled it remarkably.

Thanks to my sons Jemiah and Tory for growing to be fine young men and for their support. I'm proud of you guys.

Thanks to my mom, dad and my brothers and sisters who all helped me from going in the opposite direction.

Thanks to Larry and Linda, William and Melissa who have, over the years, learned what I was really like...and still remained my friends. Don't worry guys, the money I promised you to be my friends is coming.

Thanks to those who helped me prepare to publish this book.

Ricky, Sheila, Roy and others. And thanks Isaac for pointing me toward the internet as a way to get my word out.

Thanks to my church family, West End SDA, for being such an inspiration. What an experience. I wish everyone around the world could share in that experience. In fact, everyone can. Go to ChurchPond.com.

Thanks to my Pastor and his wife, Calvin and Wynona Preston, for their awesome ministry.

And, I especially like to thank Pastor Preston for allowing me to teach and be an integral part of his evangelism efforts. It's an honor and privilege I hold dear to my heart.

Now, to the Master Teacher, the Holy Spirit, I also thank *You* for including me in *Your* evangelism efforts. You've equipped me well. You've inspired me immensely. Please continue to reach out to others through me. The work will do me good.

****

To all of you that have, over the years, insisted that I "write all that stuff down" that I was teaching, this book is dedicated to you. Thanks!

Printed in Great Britain
by Amazon

22347009R00066